UNICORN
ACTIVITY BOOK FOR KIDS

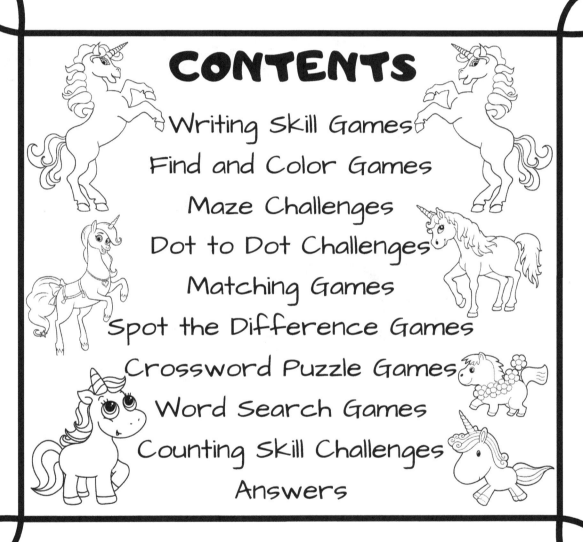

CONTENTS

THIS COLORING BOOK BELONGS TO:

Writing Skill Game:

U u is for
Unicorn

Find and Color Game:

Can you color the unicorn with their assigned color?

1 - pink	3 - red	5 - yellow
2 - violet	4 - orange	6 - blue

Maze Challenge:

Can you help the unicorn to find the way to the castle?

castle

Dot to dots challenge:
Can you connect the dots to create a charming unicorn?

Matching Test:

Can you encircle the correct
unicorn's shadow?

Spot the Difference Game:
Can you find and encircle the difference?

Crossword Puzzle Game:
Can you guess the hidden letters?

Word Search Challenge:

Can you find
the 5 unicorn words?

```
U  L  F  L  P  D  U  U  D  J
N  U  T  D  O  H  N  N  Z  V
I  N  R  T  L  F  I  I  H  Z
C  I  K  B  N  G  C  C  I  U
O  C  E  V  R  O  O  O  E  K
R  O  G  L  T  Z  R  R  E  D
N  R  C  X  Z  A  N  N  H  E
U  N  I  C  O  R  N  G  F  N
M  C  I  L  Q  P  O  X  V  Q
P  Q  Q  X  O  W  V  P  N  E
```

UNICORN   UNICORN   UNICORN

UNICORN   UNICORN

Counting Skills Challenge:

Can you count how many unicorns?

Writing Skill Game: Can you draw the capital letter U?

Writing Skill Game: Can you draw the small letter u?

Writing Skill Game:

Can you help the unicorn to get the sweets?

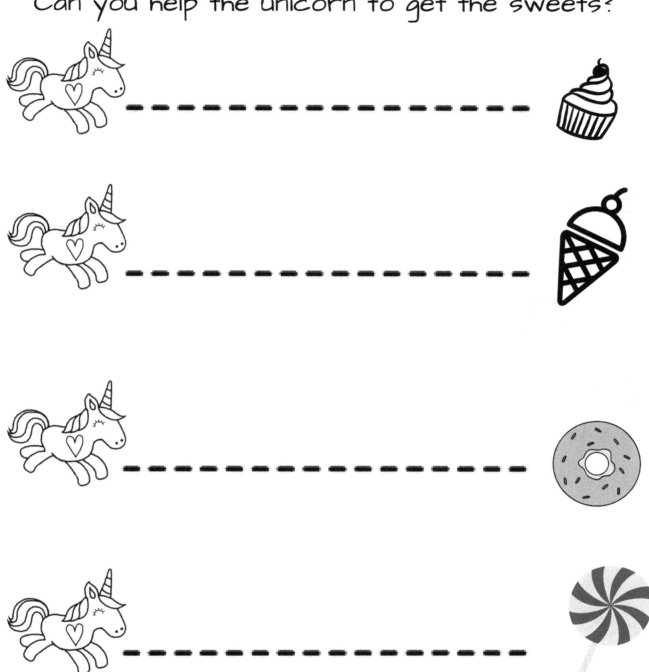

Writing Skill Game:

Can you help the unicorn to find the way to her friends?

Writing Skill Game:

Can you help the unicorn to find the way to the castle?

Writing Skill Game:

Can you help the baby unicorns tracing the lines to create shapes?

Writing Skill Game:

Can you guess the correct hidden letters?

| U | | I | | O | | N |

| S | | | A | | R |

| | O | O | |

| C | | O | | | D |

| R | | I | | B | | W |

Writing Skill Game:

Can you guess the correct hidden letters?

U		I		O	N

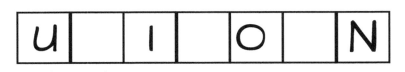

C		P	A		E

C		K	

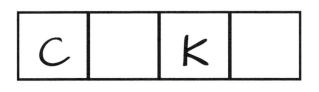

D		N		T

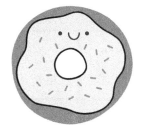

I		E	R	A	

Writing Skill Game:

Can you guess the correct hidden letters?

U		I		O		N

M		R		A		D

F			I		Y

D		A		O		

P		I		C		S

Find and Color Game:

Which one is the unicorn?

Find and Color Game:
Can you color the unicorn with their assigned color?

1 - red   3 - yellow   5 - blue   7 - pink

2 - orange 4 - green   6 - violet 8 - white

Find and Color Game:
Where is the unicorn?

Find and Color Game:

Which one is the unicorn?

Find and Color Game:
Can you color the unicorn with their assigned color?

1 - violet   3 - yellow   5 - red

2 - pink   4 - orange   6 - blue

Find and Color Game:

Where are the 2 unicorns?

Find and Color Game:
Can you color the unicorn with their assigned color?

1 - pink   3 - yellow   5 - blue

2 - violet   4 - orange   6 - red

Find and Color Game:

Which one is the unicorn?

Find and Color Game:

Where are the 3 unicorns?

Maze Challenge:
Which path should
the unicorn take
way to her
friends?

Maze Challenge:

Can you help the unicorn to get the ice cream?

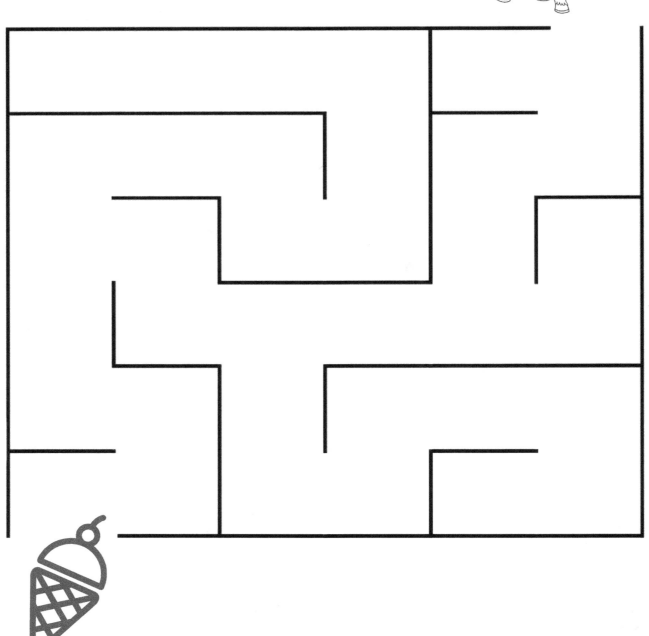

Maze Challenge:

Can you help the unicorn to get the cupcake?

Maze Challenge:

Can you help the unicorn and the fairy to find their way to the magic land?

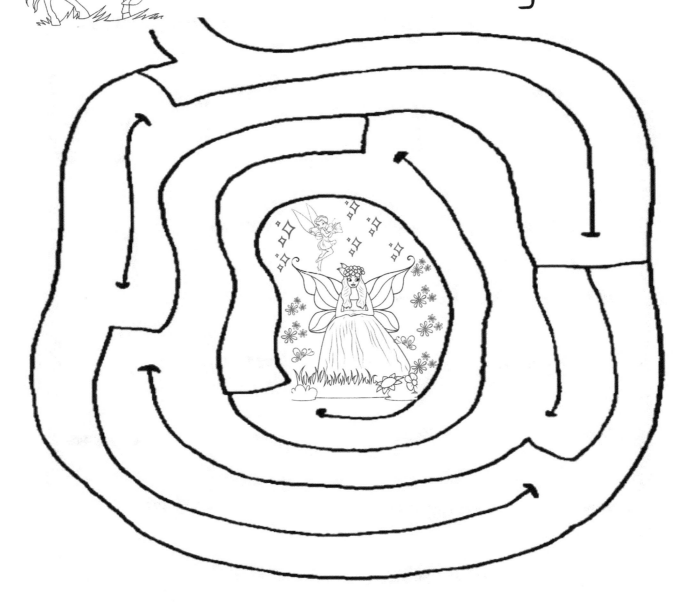

Maze Challenge: Can you help the flying unicorn and her friends to get the magic wand?

Maze Challenge:

Can you help the unicorn
to get the cake?

Maze Challenge: Can you guide the unicorn to get the gift?

Maze Challenge: Can you help the the unicorn to find the way to the rainbow clouds?

Can you help the unicorn
to save the princess?

Dot to dots challenge:

Can you connect the dots to create a cute unicorn?

Dot to dots challenge:
Can you connect the dots to create
an adorable unicorn?

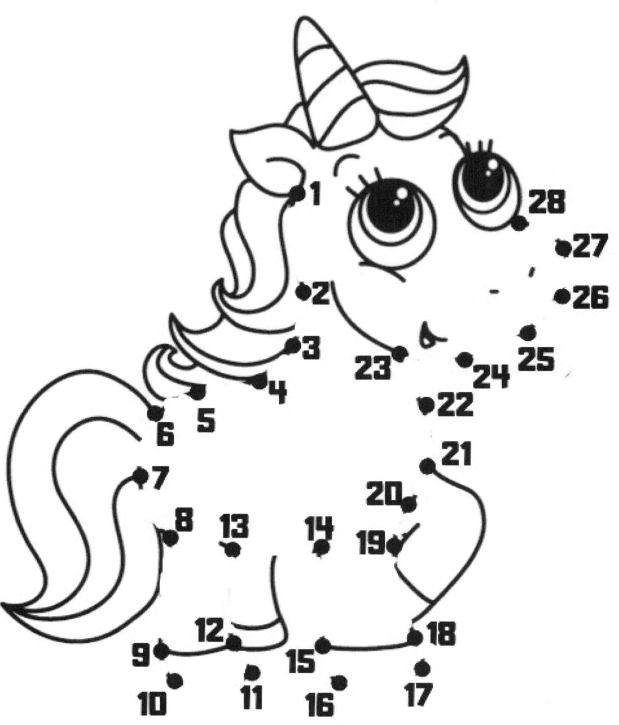

Dot to dots challenge:
Can you connect the dots to create a pretty unicorn?

Dot to dots challenge:
Can you connect the dots to create a flying unicorn?

Dot to dots challenge:

Can you connect the dots to create a lovely unicorn?

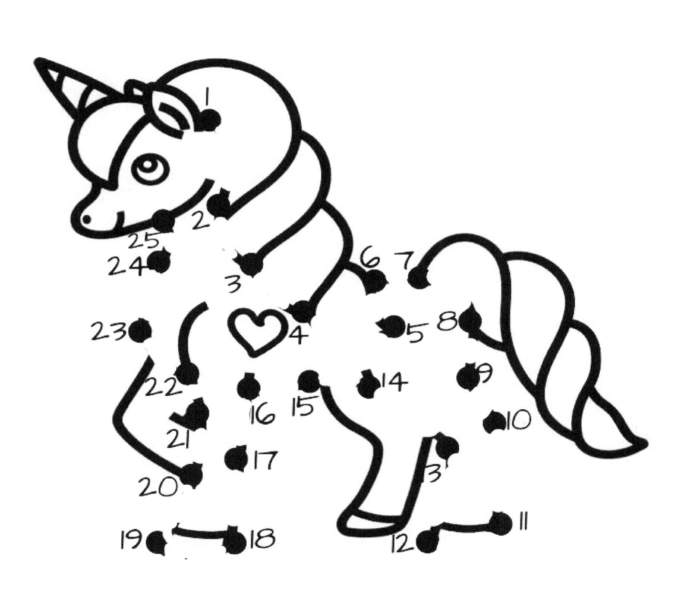

Dot to dots challenge:
Can you connect the dots to create a gorgeous unicorn?

Dot to dots challenge:
Can you connect
the dots to create
a magical unicorn?

32

33

31 30

34 29

28
27

23 26
24 25
22

35 21

20 19
10 18
11 17
36 12 16
13 15
8 9 14

37

7

38

6

39 5

4

3

2

1

Dot to dots challenge:

Can you connect the dots to create a fascinating unicorn?

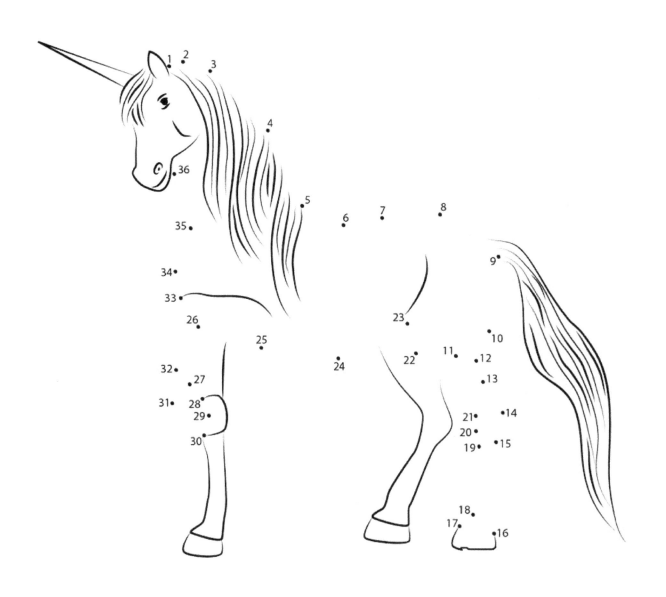

Dot to dots challenge:
Can you connect the dots to create a charming unicorn?

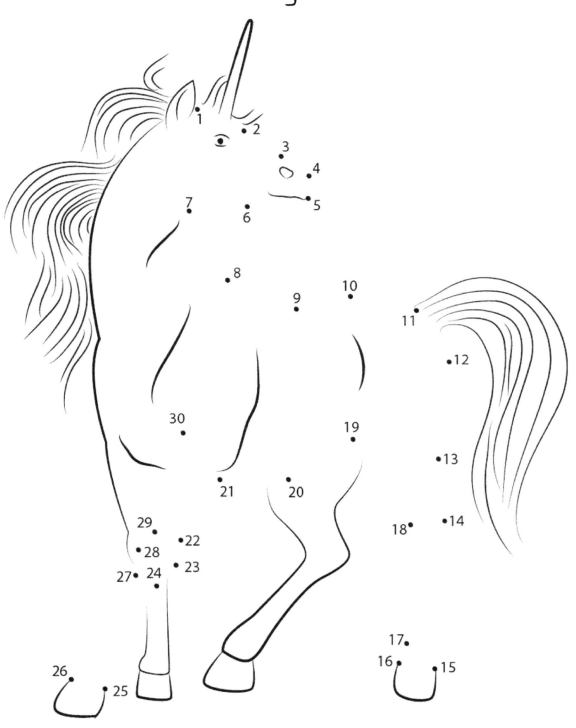

Matching Test:
Can you draw a line from each picture to the matching word?

moon

rainbow

unicorn

heart

star

Matching Test:
Can you draw a line to match the correct unicorn's shadow?

Matching Test:

Can you draw a line from each picture to the matching word?

cupcake

cake

unicorn

donut

ice cream

Matching Test:
Can you encircle which two baby unicorns are twins?

Matching Test:

Can you draw a line from each picture to the matching word?

dragon

unicorn

dinosaur

Matching Test:
Can you encircle the 3 matching unicorns ?

Let's party!

Matching Test:

Can you draw a line to match the unicorn parents to their children?

Matching Test:

Can you encircle the two unicorns that are exactly the same?

Matching Test:

Can you draw a line from each picture to the matching word?

mermaid

princess

unicorn

fairy

Spot the Difference Game:
Which one is different from the others?

Spot the Difference Game:

Can you spot the
2 differences
between the
pictures?

Spot the Difference Game:

Which one is different from the others?

Spot the Difference Game:

Can you find and encircle the 3 differences between the pictures?

Spot the Difference Game:

Which one is different from the others?

Spot the Difference Game:

Can you spot the 4 differences ?

Spot the Difference Game:

Which one is different from the others?

Spot the Difference Game:

Can you encircle the 5 differences?

Spot the Difference Game:

Which one is different from the others?

Crossword Puzzle Game:
Can you guess the hidden letters?

Crossword Puzzle Game:
Can you guess the hidden letters?

Crossword Puzzle Game:
Can you guess the hidden letters?

Crossword Puzzle Game:

Can you guess the hidden letters?

```
                      S
    B U           R       Y
              R
      C           N
F     W
      N           W
```

Crossword Puzzle Game:

Can you guess the
hidden letters?

Crossword Puzzle Game:
Can you guess the hidden letters?

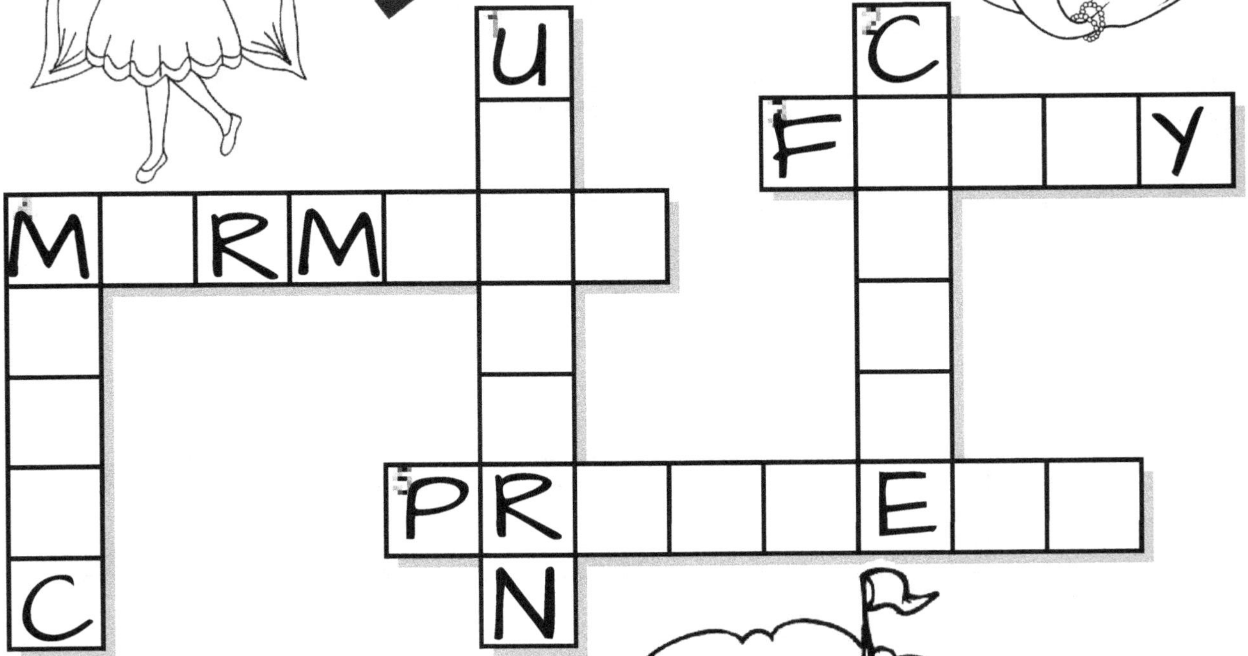

U

F C Y

M R M

P R N E

C

Crossword Puzzle Game:

Can you guess the hidden letters?

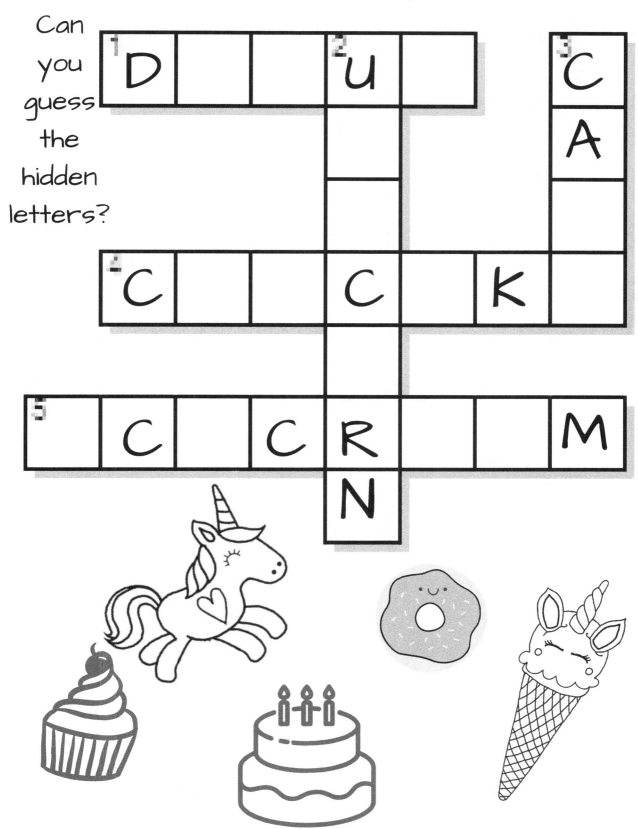

Crossword Puzzle Game:

Can you guess the hidden letters?

Crossword Puzzle Game:
Can you guess the hidden letters?

Word Search Challenge:

Can you look for the 6 magical words?

```
F  P  W  J  K  C  A  U  P  H
G  F  Q  R  S  B  Z  N  M  X
W  N  X  K  T  N  K  I  O  B
B  C  X  X  A  G  R  C  O  D
Y  L  Z  E  R  A  G  O  N  I
G  O  G  N  N  E  K  R  D  V
D  U  U  L  W  S  U  N  T  S
I  D  D  S  H  L  K  Q  C  X
R  A  I  N  B  O  W  D  A  W
C  P  H  Z  R  G  E  R  I  S
```

UNICORN	CLOUD	RAINBOW
STAR	SUN	MOON

Word Search Challenge:

Can you search for
the 6 words?

S B C A W I P G S E

T U J C Y X D G H K

F T U V F G R M D I

A T N O L G A A K E

I E I A O N G G B P

R R C N W M O I C N

Y F O H E A N C A U

D L R W R V F E A Z

W Y N E N U L O S W

P D D A E Z Y Y N R

UNICORN   FAIRY   BUTTERFLY
DRAGONFLY FLOWER   MAGIC

Word Search Challenge:

Can you find the 6 magical creature words?

```
G A K F T Q Y U T J
D Y C P P C H N Y Q
R S M E R M A I D P
A M F T I T R C Y Y
G Y A H N Q C O G Z
O X I R C T A R Z Q
N J R E E N S N P P
V R Y F S X T R B U
U X K U S S L Q E I
W R Y P E F E S M E
```

UNICORN   MERMAID   PRINCESS

FAIRY   CASTLE   DRAGON

Word Search Challenge:

Can you look for the 7 animal words?

```
F  P  U  N  I  C  O  R  N  R
S  P  L  K  E  O  J  T  F  H
H  J  M  L  L  X  N  U  Z  I
G  U  G  P  E  L  K  R  A  N
V  Y  I  B  P  I  G  I  V  O
W  J  R  Z  H  O  J  N  V  C
B  R  A  E  A  N  W  G  W  E
F  Q  F  B  N  A  Q  I  M  R
L  E  F  R  T  I  G  E  R  O
Q  I  E  A  Q  R  C  K  Z  S
```

UNICORN   GIRAFFE   ZEBRA
ELEPHANT   RHINOCEROS LION
TIGER

Word Search Challenge:

Can you look for the
7 delicious words?

```
M  H  N  W  C  I  W  S  Q  D
D  C  Z  X  M  O  Z  D  Q  O
C  A  C  I  T  R  D  D  I  N
U  K  Q  I  I  U  G  Q  N  U
P  E  J  C  R  E  A  M  O  T
C  M  P  E  A  C  U  Y  D  L
A  G  Q  S  I  G  M  S  H  S
K  X  D  P  I  Z  Z  A  B  U
E  Z  G  Y  O  C  Y  T  X  K
U  N  I  C  O  R  N  Q  N  U
```

UNICORN   DONUT   ICE

CREAM   CAKE   PIZZA

CUPCAKE

Word Search Challenge:

Can you search for the
unicorn's part of the body?

```
O D W I N G S W M Q
J J J E O L O A O S
O Z F E E T M V A R
Y Q F V F F L M P V
T A I L E Y E S C H
G T M N N N K H E F
V H O S G E U O F R
N J U N I C O R N P
V S T P Z K F N N X
Q I H X W E S N U Y
```

UNICORN   HORN   WINGS

TAIL   EYES   FEET

MOUTH   NECK

Word Search Challenge:

Can you find the 7 different shapes?

```
D  N  W  S  X  N  P  H  N  R
Q  R  T  Q  V  N  L  Z  S  E
Z  A  P  U  S  X  K  S  Q  C
U  D  I  A  M  O  N  D  A  T
N  J  N  R  T  V  R  W  Z  A
I  R  T  E  E  H  Z  Y  G  N
C  I  R  C  L  E  B  U  Z  G
O  B  D  A  R  A  M  S  Q  L
R  S  S  T  A  R  Q  Z  I  E
N  J  Z  G  R  T  P  B  X  C
```

UNICORN   STAR   HEART
CIRCLE   SQUARE   DIAMOND
RECTANGLE

Word Search Challenge:

Can you search for the
5 magical creatures?

P B F A I R Y R Y Z E N

E S D B Y R Y L S O

S U X C I K T U O G

O S S J L S J Q C A

H S E V A U I X B R

U N I C O R N U F D

A Z X F N W R W R G

X I X R I I I G S B

L I G F Z T R W Z J

Y N N F L G L P P X

_____

UNICORN   PRINCESS   FAIRY
DRAGON   CASTLE

Word Search Challenge:

Can you search for the 6 creatures?

```
Y  D  R  A  G  O  N  F  L  Y
J  M  E  R  M  A  I  D  X  U
Z  H  U  M  R  G  F  D  Y  V
T  C  G  E  F  Q  E  C  P  Q
N  F  K  Z  R  P  Y  Y  B  L
M  V  B  K  F  V  Z  C  U  D
R  U  A  S  O  N  I  D  J  R
U  N  I  C  O  R  N  K  H  E
S  O  R  E  C  O  N  I  H  R
Q  P  E  G  A  S  U  S  P  G
```

UNICORN   DINOSAUR   DRAGONFLY

RHINOCEROS MERMAID   PEGASUS

Counting Skills Challenge:

How many unicorns are there?

Counting Skills Challenge:

Can you count how many baby unicorns are there?

Counting Skills Challenge:

How many unicorns are there?

Counting Skills Challenge:

Can you color the star of the correct count?

Counting Skills Challenge:

Can you color the cloud of the correct count?

Counting Skills Challenge:

Can you draw a line to the star of the correct corresponding count?

Counting Skills Challenge:

Can you draw a line to the cloud of the correct corresponding count?

Counting Skills Challenge:

Can you write inside the star the correct count
of the flying baby unicorns?

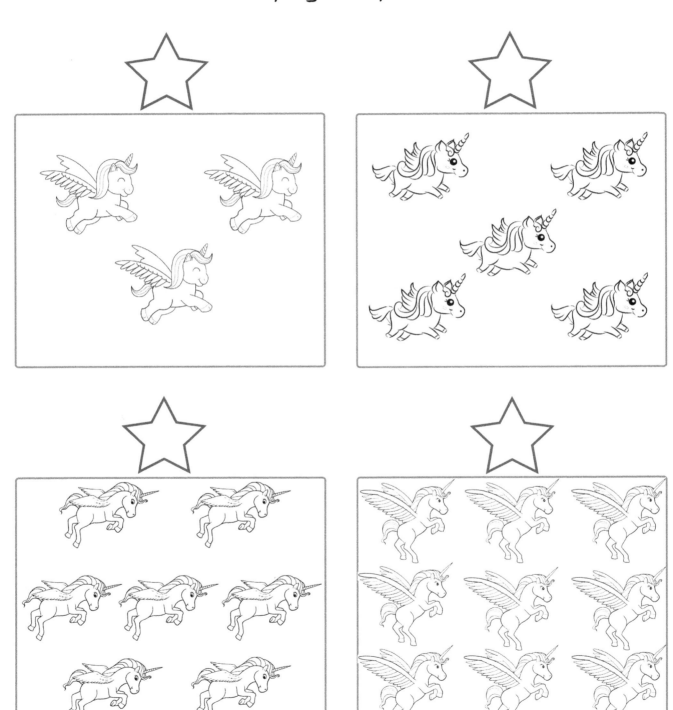

Counting Skills Challenge:

Can you write inside the cloud the correct count
of the flying unicorns?

Answers

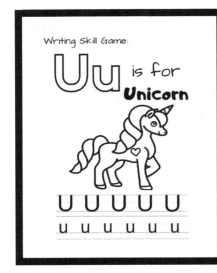

Writing Skill Game:

Uu is for **Unicorn**

U U U U U
u u u u u u

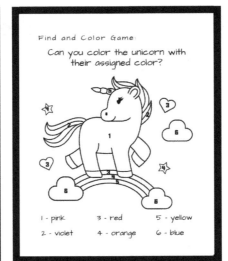

Find and Color Game:
Can you color the unicorn with
their assigned color?

1 - pink   3 - red   5 - yellow
2 - violet   4 - orange   6 - blue

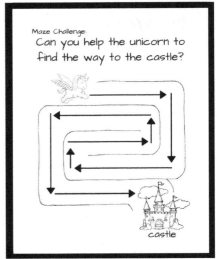

Maze Challenge:
Can you help the unicorn to
find the way to the castle?

castle

Dot to dots challenge:
Can you connect the dots to create
a charming unicorn?

Matching Test:
Can you encircle the correct
unicorn's shadow?

Spot the Difference Game:
Can you find and encircle the difference?

Crossword Puzzle Game:
Can you guess the hidden letters?

M O O N
        R
    S T A R
        I
  U N I C O R N
        B
        O
      C L O U D
        W

Word Search Challenge:
Can you find
the 5 unicorn words?

U L F L P D U U D J
U N T D O H N N Z V
N I R T L F I I H Z
I C K B N G C C I U
C O E V R O O O E K
O R G L T Z R R E D
R R C X Z A N N H E
U N I C O R N G F N
M C I L Q P O X V Q
P Q Q X O W V P N E

UNICORN   UNICORN   UNICORN
UNICORN   UNICORN

Counting Skills Challenge:

Can you count how many unicorns?

3

Answers for Writing Skill Games

Writing Skill Game: Can you draw the capital letter U?

Uu

U U U U U
U U U U U
U U U U U
U U U U U
U U U U U

Writing Skill Game: Can you draw the small letter U?

Uu

u u u u u
u u u u u
u u u u u
u u u u u

Writing Skill Game:

Can you help the unicorn to get the sweets?

Writing Skill Game:

Can you help the unicorn to find the way to her friends?

Writing Skill Game:

Can you help the unicorn to find the way to the castle?

Writing Skill Game:

Can you help the baby unicorns tracing the lines to create shapes?

Writing Skill Game:

Can you guess the correct hidden letters?

UNICORN
STAR
MOON
CLOUD
RAINBOW

Writing Skill Game:

Can you guess the correct hidden letters?

UNICORN
CUPCAKE
CAKE
DONUT
ICECREAM

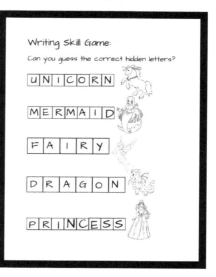

Writing Skill Game:

Can you guess the correct hidden letters?

UNICORN
MERMAID
FAIRY
DRAGON
PRINCESS

Answers for Find and Color Games

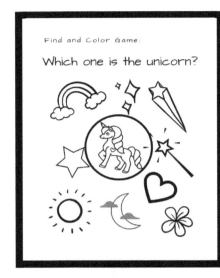

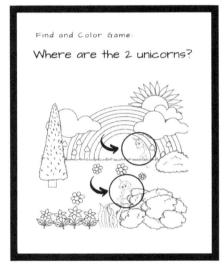

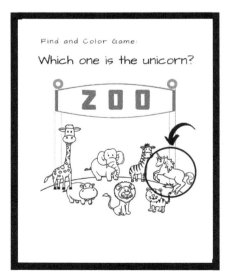

Answers for Mazes Challenges

Maze Challenge:
Which path should the unicorn take way to her friends?

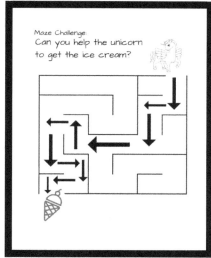

Maze Challenge:
Can you help the unicorn to get the ice cream?

Maze Challenge:
Can you help the unicorn to get the cupcake?

Maze Challenge:
Can you help the unicorn and the fairy to find their way to the magic land?

Maze Challenge: Can you help the flying unicorn and her friends to get the magic wand?

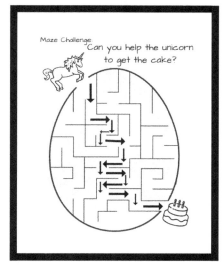

Maze Challenge:
Can you help the unicorn to get the cake?

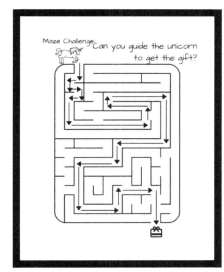

Maze Challenge: Can you guide the unicorn to get the gift?

Maze Challenge: Can you help the the unicorn to find the way to the rainbow clouds?

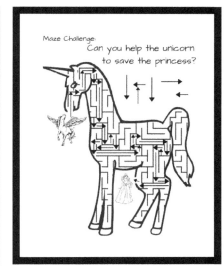

Maze Challenge:
Can you help the unicorn to save the princess?

Answers for Dot to Dot Challenges

Dot to dots challenge:
Can you connect the dots to create a cute unicorn?

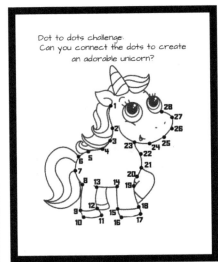

Dot to dots challenge:
Can you connect the dots to create an adorable unicorn?

Dot to dots challenge:
Can you connect the dots to create a pretty unicorn?

Dot to dots challenge:
Can you connect the dots to create a flying unicorn?

Dot to dots challenge:
Can you connect the dots to create a fascinating unicorn?

Dot to dots challenge:
Can you connect the dots to create a gorgeous unicorn?

Dot to dots challenge:
Can you connect the dots to create a magical unicorn?

Dot to dots challenge:
Can you connect the dots to create a lovely unicorn?

Dot to dots challenge:
Can you connect the dots to create a charming unicorn?

Answers for Matching Games

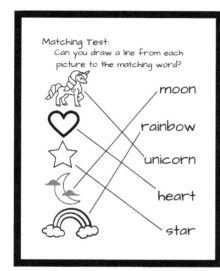

Matching Test:
Can you draw a line from each picture to the matching word?

moon

rainbow

unicorn

heart

star

Matching Test:
Can you draw a line to match the correct unicorn's shadow?

Matching Test:
Can you draw a line from each picture to the matching word?

cupcake

cake

unicorn

donut

ice cream

Matching Test:
Can you encircle which two baby unicorns are twins?

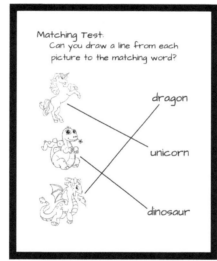

Matching Test:
Can you draw a line from each picture to the matching word?

dragon

unicorn

dinosaur

Matching Test:
Can you encircle the 3 matching unicorns?

Let's party!

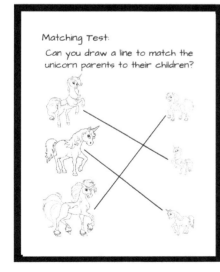

Matching Test:
Can you draw a line to match the unicorn parents to their children?

Matching Test:
Can you encircle the two unicorns that are exactly the same?

Matching Test:
Can you draw a line from each picture to the matching word?

mermaid

princess

unicorn

fairy

Answers for Spot the Difference GAmes

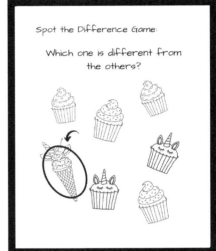

Answers for Crossword Puzzle

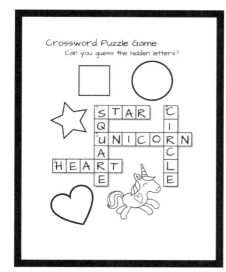

Crossword Puzzle Game:
Can you guess the hidden letters?

STAR
CIRCLE
SQUARE
UNICORN
HEART

Crossword Puzzle Game:
Can you guess the hidden letters?

WH
UNICORN
WINGS
HORN
FEET
EYES
TAIL

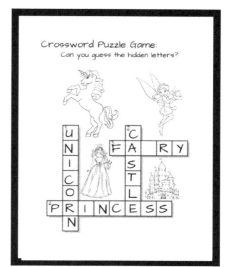

Crossword Puzzle Game:
Can you guess the hidden letters?

UNICORN
CASTLE
FAIRY
PRINCESS

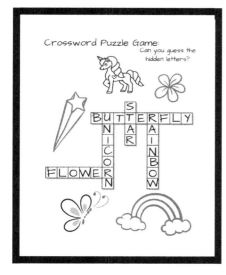

Crossword Puzzle Game:
Can you guess the hidden letters?

BUTTERFLY
STAR
UNICORN
RAINBOW
FLOWER

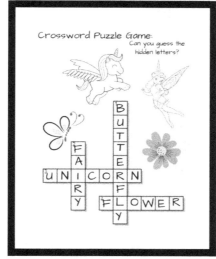

Crossword Puzzle Game:
Can you guess the hidden letters?

BUTTERFLY
FAIRY
UNICORN
FLOWER

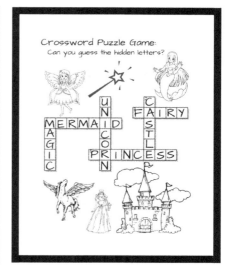

Crossword Puzzle Game:
Can you guess the hidden letters?

UNICORN
CASTLE
FAIRY
MERMAID
MAGIC
PRINCESS

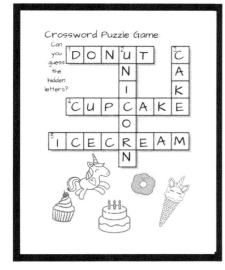

Crossword Puzzle Game:
Can you guess the hidden letters?

DONUT
CAKE
UNICORN
CUPCAKE
ICECREAM

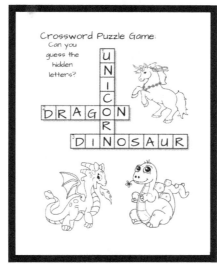

Crossword Puzzle Game:
Can you guess the hidden letters?

UNICORN
DRAGON
DINOSAUR

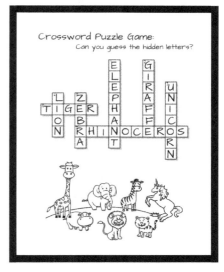

Crossword Puzzle Game:
Can you guess the hidden letters?

ELEPHANT
GIRAFFE
LION
TIGER
ZEBRA
UNICORN
RHINOCEROS

Answers for Word Search Games

Word Search Challenge:
Can you look for the 6 magical words?

UNICORN   CLOUD   RAINBOW
STAR   SUN   MOON

Word Search Challenge:
Can you search for the 6 words?

UNICORN   FAIRY   BUTTERFLY
DRAGONFLY   FLOWER   MAGIC

Word Search Challenge:
Can you find the 6 magical creature words?

UNICORN   MERMAID   PRINCESS
FAIRY   CASTLE   DRAGON

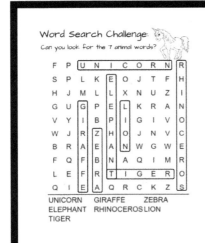

Word Search Challenge:
Can you look for the 7 animal words?

UNICORN   GIRAFFE   ZEBRA
ELEPHANT   RHINOCEROS   LION
TIGER

Word Search Challenge:
Can you look for the 7 delicious words?

UNICORN   DONUT   ICE
CREAM   CAKE   PIZZA
CUPCAKE

Word Search Challenge:
Can you search for the unicorn's part of the body?

UNICORN   HORN   WINGS
TAIL   EYES   FEET
MOUTH   NECK

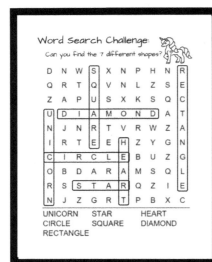

Word Search Challenge:
Can you find the 7 different shapes?

UNICORN   STAR   HEART
CIRCLE   SQUARE   DIAMOND
RECTANGLE

Word Search Challenge:
Can you search for the 5 magical creatures?

UNICORN   PRINCESS   FAIRY
DRAGON   CASTLE

Word Search Challenge:
Can you search for the 6 creatures?

UNICORN   DINOSAUR   DRAGONFLY
RHINOCEROS   MERMAID   PEGASUS

Answers for Counting Skill Challenges

Counting Skills Challenge:
How many unicorns are there?

4

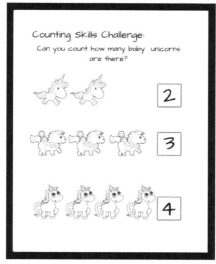

Counting Skills Challenge:
Can you count how many baby unicorns are there?

2
3
4

Counting Skills Challenge:
How many unicorns are there?

3
4
5

Counting Skills Challenge:
Can you color the star of the correct count?

1
2
3

Counting Skills Challenge:
Can you color the cloud of the correct count?

3
4
5

Counting Skills Challenge:
Can you draw a line to the star of the correct corresponding count?

5
3
4

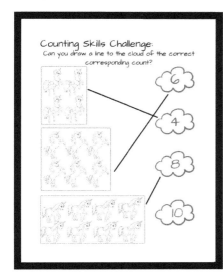

Counting Skills Challenge:
Can you draw a line to the cloud of the correct corresponding count?

6
4
8
10

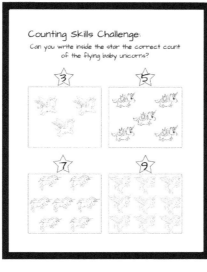

Counting Skills Challenge:
Can you write inside the star the correct count of the flying baby unicorns?

3
5
7
9

Counting Skills Challenge:
Can you write inside the cloud the correct count of the flying unicorns?

4
6
8
9